The Weight Of Remembering

Echoes of Love, Loss, and the Time In Between

Samriddhi Agarwal

BookLeaf
Publishing

India | USA | UK

Made with ❤ on the BookLeaf Publishing Platform
www.bookleafpub.in
www.bookleafpub.com

Dedication

To the love that shaped me, the memories that haunt me, and the moments that linger—etched in time, in places, in the hearts of those who remember.

For every soul who has loved and lost, for every echo that refuses to fade, and for the unspoken stories carried by the wind, the sea, and the stars.

Preface

Memory is a quiet weight we carry—sometimes a comfort, sometimes a burden, always there, pressing against our hearts in moments of stillness. This collection of poems is born from that weight, from the echoes of love that refuse to fade, from the spaces between what was and what remains.

Love, loss, longing—these are not just personal experiences, but universal ones. We all leave pieces of ourselves in the people we love, in the places we call home, in the fleeting instants that define us. This book is for those who have ever held on too tightly, let go too late, or found themselves caught between remembering and moving on.

Each poem is a whisper, a thread in the vast tapestry of human emotion, woven with both sorrow and beauty. May these words find a home in your heart, offering solace in shared experience and a quiet understanding that even in loss, there is poetry

Acknowledgements

This book would not exist without the people, places, and moments that have shaped me—those who have stayed, those who have left, and those who remain in the quiet corners of my memory.

To the love that inspired these words, whether near or far, tangible or lost in time—thank you for teaching me the depth of feeling, the beauty of connection, and the ache of absence.

To the poets, dreamers, and storytellers who have come before me—your words have been both a lighthouse and a mirror, guiding me through my own reflections.

I am endlessly grateful to my family and friends, who have held space for my words and emotions, offering unwavering support, patience, and understanding.

And to you, dear reader—thank you for carrying these poems with you. Whether they echo your own story or simply touch a quiet place in your heart, I hope they remind you that you are not alone in your remembering.

1. Red

Blades, needles, and paper cuts pierce your skin,
Slashing, leaving traces of crimson within.
A scarlet trail drips, easing the ache,
A fleeting remedy for the pain it takes.
You breathe again; a strange relief,
The weight dissolves, giving way to peace.
The tears, don't let them fall—hold them tight,
Feel the breeze like the sting of liquid's flight.
Blurring your vision, you drift to the sky,
Gravity fades as you say goodbye.
The pain's gone now; you're finally free,
The red brought you here, the red set you free.

2. Exhausted

It's exhausting to live—
Smile and wave,
Feel hollow,
Move forward,
Though every step pulls me deeper.

It's exhausting to talk—
Where and what,
Words unravel,
Each syllable stripping me bare.

It's exhausting to continue,
When all I want is to stop.

No pause, no relief—
The grind goes on,
The camera stays on.
The world spins on,
The mask stays on.

Smile for them. Be happy for them.
That's the script. That's the role.
But I am done.

No more smiles. No more words.
No more pretending. No more weight.

I will stop—
And what then?

3. Memories

The sweet, salty, tangled threads of thought,
The guiding force behind all we've sought.

The fuel that drives our joy and fears,
The echoes of our passing years.

Memories are a bizarre thing to me—
What do you mean it happened in 2003?

How do I still taste that apple pie,
Yet can't recall the reason why?

They shape the life we've loved and lived,
The people who took and those who give.

Some left halfway, fading fast,
Some still hold my hand steadfast.

Some I wish I'd never met,
Some I can't seem to forget.

Happy or sad, they hold it all,
The rise, the fall, the standing tall.
A lesson, a scar, a fleeting glance,
A second chance—or just a trance.

I think it's all philosophy,
Or else why would I still see
The gifts that Santa left for me?

Memories—both blessing and curse,
A beautiful weight, for better or worse.
And yet, despite the joy and ache,
I thank the Lord for all they make.

4. The Month of Feb

The month of love, of joy, of fate,
Where hearts find hearts, and soul meets mate.

A time when love is in the air,
With whispered words and moments rare.

Yet, February, you stand so torn,
A month of love, a month I mourn.

I lost my love, yet love was found,
My parents' hearts in you were bound.

I found friendship in your days,
Yet lost my heart in unseen ways.

A tangle of joy, a touch of sorrow,
Do I smile today or weep tomorrow?

If given a choice, I'd love once more,
Despite the wounds my heart once bore.

And you know which month I'd choose again?
The month of Feb, through joy and pain.

5. Tired

I am tired.
Breathe in.
Breathe out.
Still tired.

Hi, good morning.
I am tired.

College, classes,
Lunch, meet with masses—
I am tired.

"How was your day?"
Exhausting.
"Plans for the weekend?"
Survive.

I am tired of this.
Tired of life.

Tired of moving, yet standing still.
Tired of being here,
chasing there.

Tired of—
Emotions.
Expectations.

What to say, what to silence.
What to do, what to bury.
How to sit.
How to behave.
How to live.

Achieve this.
Achieve that.

I am done.
No hi.
No bye.
Just done.

I am tired.

6. Last Night

Last night, I almost died,
Almost whispered my goodbyes.

It wasn't painful, just surreal—
Like a dream I couldn't feel.

All that remained was the final step,
One breath away from the unknown depths.

Last night, I almost died,
Drowned in tears I couldn't hide.

Laughed, howled—I did it all,
Like a star about to fall.

Don't ask why.
I'm here to tell you.

Last night, a thought broke through—
My brother's voice, his laughter too.

He wanted biscuits, nothing more,
A simple task I can't ignore.

That's my cue to wait, to stay,
To push the darkness one more day.

Lord, I will see You soon,
But for now, I will continue.

7. A Conversation

A conversation beyond comprehension—
That's our task for today.

No masks, no walls, just truth,
Let the feelings spill, let them stay.

You can cry here—this space is safe.
You can laugh—joy won't fade away.

Speak or sit in silence,
Draw, sing, dance—just let it flow.
Be free. Breathe. Let go.

Please, dear child, please don't quit.
I swear, I'm right here with you.

I'll hold you steady in the storm,
I'll keep you safe, I'll see you through.

I beg you, don't give up the fight,

Even when it takes all your might.

You are strong. You are brave.
The darkness will not last.

A conversation beyond comprehension—
That's our task

8. Him

Hey you,
My sunshine and my storm.

Hey you,
The thief of my heart.
I gave you all I had,
Every piece I could spare.
You shook your head,
Took all you could,
And left me hollow.

I was shattered,
A ghost of me.
With silence carved,
So carefully.
Still, I loved you—
It felt so right.
But in my eyes,
I caused the fight.

Hey you,
Have I told you?
I love you still,
Against my will.
Since day one,
And till I fade,
Even broken,
I'm unafraid.

Hey you,
Why did you do it?
Why break someone
All I wanted—was that a crime?
A piece of peace, a love sublime.

I don't understand feelings,
Not like you do.

I carry hate,
Yet somehow,
None for you.

Why?
Hey you.

9. Make it Stop

The pain is too much—make it stop,
I'd rather wither, break, and rot.
I've screamed, I've bled, I've begged, I've cried,
Tried to numb, but still, it pries.
Happy, angry, hollow too,
Tell me—what else must I do?
It stabs, then sneers, a twisted art,
Like a dagger from the ones with heart.
Horrid thoughts begin to swarm,
A raging storm, a howling form.
The clover wilts, its promise dies,
Hope now whispers empty lies.
The pain is too much—make it stop.

10. Am I Fake

Am I fake, or am I real?
It's too late to feel surreal.

I am inclined to lie,
Lay low and die.

I feel fake, I feel surreal.
Happiness is just a spinning wheel.

Round and round, never mine,
Just a trick of borrowed time.

You are happy with no brains,
You are happy when it rains.

I watch, I wait, I fade, I fall—
Does it even matter at all?

I do not exist, I do not persist,
I was never meant for this.

I choose to leave for a short while,
Even that feels so futile.

I will go soon—miss me then.
Call me at noon.

Call me.

Then.

11. Stay Away

Blood-red screams, deafening loud,
Echoing storms, no light, no shroud.

I claw, I fight, yet drown the same,
A war inside—no end, no name.
The urge to go, to disappear,
To push away all who come near.

Stay away—it's toxic, vile,
A sickness that festers, mile by mile.
I am broken beyond repair,
But that's not even my worst despair.

Like it or not, the truth still stands—
I am not someone to hold your hand.

I am the rot, the spoiled slice,
Cut me away, don't think twice.
STAY AWAY, I beg of you,
This place is dark—this hell is true.

No angels here, no fairy light,
Only black and red, only blight.
Rhyme scheme can go to hell,
I'll just say it—you'll do well.

Please, do well.
STAY AWAY, I beg of you.

I am not someone you should choose.
This world is dead, this heart is cracked,
Even Lucifer flinches when I look back.

12. Do I have a future?

Do I have a future?

I never thought I'd make it here,
Beyond the pain, beyond the fear.

Should I try? Will I survive?
What does it mean to feel alive?

What's it like to dream and grow,
To chase the highs, to ride the low?

To have a list, to make a mark,
To spark a flame inside the dark.

Strike the checks, not your skin,
Let the light come seeping in.

What if there's more I've yet to see?
What if the best is meant for me?

I wonder how the sunrise feels,
If laughter heals, if time reveals.

Maybe life's a fleeting track,
But the clouds, they've got my back.

13. Sleep

Sleep is the happy pill,
The friend that never will
Let me down,
Stress me out,
Make me wish to black out.

Sleep is my poison,
My magic potion
The one that demands my full devotion.

A drug I crave,
A ghost I chase.

I long for sleep, I beg for it.
But.
Every story has two sides.
The more I want it, the more it runs.

A love unbalanced was then unfurled—one is all in, one
is all out.

The harder I chase, the further it fades.
Sleep taunts me, teases me, mocks me daily
Slipping through my fingers, and laughing in the dark
alley.

I let it go, yet I still wait,
Loving the game, addicted to the ache.
I love sleep—it wrecks me, it saves me.

It owns me, yet denies me.
A toxic need

.

A necessary vice.
A pleasure just out of reach.

14. Scared of Love

I am scared of love—
The promises it makes,
The hopes it gives,
Like lullabies sung before the storm.

I have seen the other side,
The silent wars, the sleepless nights,
The sacrifices that leave you hollow,

The pain that lingers like an echo.
I am scared of love—
The idea of unlocking the dungeon,
Letting someone in,
Handing them the hammer to break my walls,
Hoping they rebuild instead of wreck.

I know I don't deserve it,
Or maybe it's love that doesn't deserve me.

It is heaven with a hell in it—

A paradise with fire at its core.

Love is scared.
Love is sacred.

Just a shift of letters,
Yet it changes - everything.

15. The Weight of Wishing

I wish to live,
I wish to laugh,
I wish to feel,
I wish to share.

But my voice lies buried deep—
A whisper lost beneath the weight of air.
I need to find it, but how?
All I know is—I need it now.

I wish to die,
I wish to bleed,
I wish to shrink into a tiny seed.
But the world will not bend,
Will not pause,
Will not heed.

I write with all my might,
Hoping someone, somewhere,

Sees the fight.
Cuts and bruises on my skin—
Now inked on paper, whisper-thin.

I wish to swim, then let myself drown,
For heavy, they say, is the crown.

Yet I hesitate, caught between light and shade,
Between the choice to fade,
Or to stay.

16. The Morning After I Was Gone

The morning after I was gone,
The sun still rose, bold and bright,
No stars lingered in the sky,
And birds took flight without a pause.

The world turned like it always had—
Unaffected, unshaken, untouched.
The morning after I was gone,
I whispered hello to God.
He asked me why—
I had no reply.

The morning after I was gone,
The world moved on, step by step.
No rhythm skipped, no silence fell,
Only I had taken the fall.

The place was neat, the chairs in rows,
The eulogy began—

Tears rolled out, as my name rolled in.
The morning after I was gone,
Clouds cleared, the sky stood still,
No storm, no mourning winds,
No protest from the earth.

But my mother shed a single tear—
And how I wished to hold her near.

The morning after I was gone,
It was the brightest day of my life.

The sun didn't falter.
The sky didn't break.
The earth didn't stop.

Only I did.

17. The Twins I cannot trust

Anger lives within my veins,
A fire fed by endless pains.

Is happiness my twin or my fear?
A fleeting ghost that won't stay near.

Hate me, break me, tear me apart,
Just don't deceive my hollow heart.

Love's a beautiful, whispered lie,
A dagger cloaked, a watchful spy.

It lures you in with warmth so sweet,
Then leaves you begging at its feet.

No soul is selflessly kind—
Truth is the sharpest blade you'll find.

Hate is bitter, cold, and true,
Uproots the past and buries you.

Is happiness my twin or my fear?
It holds me close, then disappears.

Yet in the dark, a voice remains,
Soft as a dream, sharp as chains.

"If happiness is but a mask," it sighs,
"Tell me—who am I behind my eyes?"

18. Trust Fall

Loving someone isn't easy—it's a trust fall,
Yet I don't do trust falls, not at all.
Still, I let them in, knowing full well,
Love is a story where both rise and fall.

Why take the risk, why step so near?
For borrowed warmth that outlasts the fear.
Why let them in, why bear the weight?
Because even ghosts deserve a soulmate.

19. Blip

I felt a blip of happiness,
a day untouched by sadness.

For once, I didn't crave the end,
I laughed—full, unrestrained.

Everything made me smile,
a feeling I hadn't held in a while.

But the blip was short-lived,
a flicker, a figment—
gone before I could hold it.

I tasted joy—
God, that's addictive.

A moment free from the looming dark,
a breath untouched by sinking hearts.

Now I chase the blip,

a fleeting spark in endless mist.

It's either that or let the dark decide,
let the world choose the rest.

20. Miss Me

Miss me
That's what I say when I want you to stay.
What I mean is—I miss you, I need you, I want you to
stay.

Miss me when the world is quiet, miss me when it's too
loud.
Miss me in your sadness, miss me in your happy sounds.

Miss me when laughter feels hollow and thin,
When joy has no room for the ghost I have been.

I'm there with you—I wish to be.
Even when I'm not. Even when I won't be.

I'm there in the spaces you try to ignore,
A breath on your skin, a knock at the door.
Even when absent, I wish to remain,
A flicker of light at the edge of your pain.

Miss me, I say, to the dearest ones. And you are one.
I wish you'd forget me when I go.
I wish you'd remember only the ghost.

Not the weight, not the ache.
Miss me, but only while I live.

Hey, you—
When time moves along,
Will you miss me, truly, when I am gone?

21. It's Time

The time has come.
Say your goodbyes.

Say congrats.
To those who must live without you—
you're giving them peace.

You tried to survive, didn't you?
Gasped for air,
ached for love—
and what did you get?

Longing.
Hate.
Pain.

A breathless, lonely soul.
Why settle for it?

Let it go.

Let yourself go.
Fly.

But before you leave,
bleed your goodbyes onto the page.

Let the ink whisper one last time,
a farewell carved in trembling lines.

One last act.
One final scene.

22. Hidden

A part of me is hidden,
Behind the walls, beneath the shell.
It will be the cause of my very end.

They say it's good to step into the sun,
But I have heat left to burn—
Burning me from the inside out.

Lights out, kids. It's time to sleep.
No one is allowed to weep.

Hidden—stored far away,
Away from the crowd, the noise, the world.
It only escapes when no one's around.

"Keep it hidden," I was once told.
When I trusted a kind soul,

But they said the world isn't the place for it.
The heavens won't let it stay.

Hell is where it belongs.

You'll see a pattern in these poems,
The mention of hell in me.
Wait until you see inside this soul—
Where even God is scared to be.

23. Because You Can

Why?
Do you not feel positive emotions?
How can you not be happy?

Why is it tough to smile,
Or not whine about your life?

Why are you so lost in the grey,
When life is bursting with colour each day?

Stop being petty,
Be thankful, be cheery.

Not everyone gets to live like you do,
Yet you drown in the weight of your issues.

Stop. Just stop.
Take a breath. Look around.

What is wrong, what holds you down?
Breathe. Laugh. Feel.

Not because you should—
But because you can.

24. What if

What if tonight is the last you see,
The final touch you get from me?

Come close, don't turn away,
Hold me tight—don't let me stray.

I might go far, far from here,
A place beyond, so bright, so clear.

No chains, no ties—I'm breaking free,
And yet, you still hold on to me.

What if I take you for a ride,
Southward bound, side by side?

Breathe it in, don't be scared,
Hold on tight—be prepared.

What if the earth begins to crack,

No time to run, no turning back?

Would you call your enemy,
Or cling to love and family?

What if, what if—it all must end,
Would you break, or would you bend?

25. Spark of Hope

Look alive, look at the sky
The birds are chirping, the sun shines high
A new day dawns, a brand-new start
A chance to chase what's in your heart
Lively and bubbly—that's the vibe
Don't let it slip, don't let it slide
Say hello, ask how they've been
Meet and greet—let warmth begin
The past is gone, the dark's behind
Today brings light—so let it shine
Let it stay, please, let it stay
A spark of hope in every day.